The Audit Explosion

Michael Power

DEM⊙S

First published in 1994
by
Demos
9 Bridewell Place
London EC4V 6AP
tel: 071 353 4479
fax: 071 353 4481

Paper No. 7

ISBN 1 898 309 30 2

Cover illustration by Andrzej Krause

Printed in Great Britain by
White Dove Press
London
Typesetting by Bartle & Wade Associates

We must... decide whether our object in setting up the Guardian class is to make it as happy as we can, or whether happiness is a thing we should look for in the community as whole.

Plato, *The Republic*

The people who produce this talk of change - professionals, politicians, administrators, committees, fund raisers, researchers and journalists - are all mounting a complex sociodrama for each other and their respective publics. This takes the form of shamanism: a series of conjuring tricks in which agencies are shuffled, new games invented, incantations recited, commissions, committees, laws, programmes and campaigns announced. All this to give the impression that social problems... are somehow not totally out of control. Promises and gestures can be made, anxieties can vanish away or be exorcised, people can be reassured or mesmerised.

Stanley Cohen, *Visions of Social Control*

INTRODUCTION: GENERAL THEMES

The word 'audit' is being used in the UK with growing frequency. In addition to financial audits, there are now environmental audits, value for money audits, management audits, forensic audits, data audits, intellectual property audits, medical audits, teaching audits, technology audits, stress audits, democracy audits and many others besides.[1] More generally, the spread of audits and other quality assurance initiatives means that many individuals and organisations now find themselves subject to audit for the first time and, notwithstanding protest and complaint, have come to think of themselves as auditees. Indeed there is a real sense in which 1990s Britain has become an 'audit society'.[2]

What are we to make of this explosion of 'audits'? What changes in the style of government does it characterise? Is this a distinctive phase in the life of advanced industrial societies? More critically, how can a practice whose benefits are being privately questioned as never before nevertheless come to occupy such an important role in public policy? Have alternatives to audit really become so unthinkable? Can we no longer think of accountability without elaborately detailed policing mechanisms?

This essay explores these questions and goes on to ask whether the audit explosion rests on firm intellectual and practical foundations or whether it is as much a symptom of problems as their cure. It asks whether audits deliver what they promise in the form of greater accountability, efficiency and quality or whether they in fact fuel the problems which they address by, for example, exacerbating distrust. Finally, it suggests a new agenda for balancing the aspiration for autonomy with external pressures for accountability.

The nature of the audit explosion is difficult to quantify but there are a number of indicators. The establishment of the National Audit Office and the Audit Commission in the early 1980s consolidated the audit resources of central and local government respectively, and provided an institutional focus for addressing the economy, efficiency and effectiveness of publicly funded activities. Both these organisations have expanded their work, particularly in value for money audit, bringing intensive scrutiny to many new areas such as the various elements of the criminal justice system -police, forensic science, crown prosecution and probation services.[3]

Medical and teaching institutions are also set to become subject to extensive auditing regimes. Medical audits have acquired prominence in response to a recent government white paper[4] and the newly established Higher Education Quality Council (HEQC) and its auditing activities will become increasingly influential.[5] In the field of quality assurance more generally, the British Standards Institute has successfully promoted BS5750, its standard for quality assurance, and has used it to develop the BS7750 standard for environmental management systems. The European Commission has issued a regulation for a voluntary Eco-Management and Audit scheme which closely resembles BS7750. The likely take-up of these initiatives is still unclear but it has been estimated that there is a $200 billion market to be covered by environmental consulting[6] and the number of consulting organisations in this area has risen dramatically in the last ten years.[7] The recent development of accreditation schemes for environmental auditors has provided a further stimulus.[8]

The major accounting firms grew very quickly during the 1980s. The proportion of university graduates entering traineeships with accountancy firms peaked at over 10% in 1987 and is currently running at about 8%.[9] Of this number, a majority receive their primary training in financial audit work although relatively few remain in this field. One important dimension of the UK audit explosion is that unprecedentedly large numbers of young people are being trained and socialised in the context of auditing.

In traditional financial audit the trends are less conspicuous. While the number of statutory entities requiring audit has grown steadily, it is the more intensive role of audit which is more notable. The statutory financial audit of companies has become more highly regulated and codified over the last twenty years. The Auditing Practices Committee, replaced by the Auditing Practices Board in 1991, was formed in 1976 and has produced technical guidance on a wide range of issues. Developments have been evident in two particular fields: financial regulation and charities. In the case of both fields, particular statutory initiatives have extended the role of audit. The *Financial Services Act 1986* and the *Banking Act 1987* have given auditors newly explicit responsibilities for assessing internal controls and for communicating with regulators. Many have complained that the costs of these arrangements are out of proportion to their benefits.[10] Charities have also come under renewed regulatory scrutiny. Supplementary provisions to the *Charities Act 1992*, and accounting guidance specifically tailored to the sector, reflect a determination to subject these organisations to increased financial discipline via audit.[11]

In other areas, the audit explosion has taken different forms. Safety and hazard audits in industry have grown naturally from health and safety legislation. Data audits, which originated in the United States and are less prominent in the UK, have arisen from concerns about scientific fraud.[12] UK public science will soon find itself subject to value for money, intellectual property and technology audits as government seeks both to make science accountable to its funding publics and to exploit its intellectual property base.[13]

Despite these developments, the audit explosion is only in part a quantitative story of human and financial resources committed to audit and its extension into new fields. It also concerns a qualitative shift: the spread of a distinct mentality of administrative control, a pervasive logic which has a life over and above specific practices. One crucial aspect of this is that many more individuals and organisations are coming to think of themselves as subjects of audit. To describe this logic, this essay relies upon a more oblique and lateral approach to the phenomenon of audit than quantitative methods would permit.[14]

In what follows I will make eight more or less discrete arguments:

First, that despite differences in context and meaning, there is a common thread to the new uses of the word 'audit'. Sceptics may doubt whether the proliferating usage of a single word really signifies any systematic relationship between the diverse contexts within which it is invoked. After all, audit is hardly an unambiguous concept and it could be argued that the practices to which the label is attached are in fact diverse and that they are constituted by very different bodies of knowledge. For example, it is possible to distinguish audits on the basis of their relation to the auditee. Many audits, such as in medicine, are conceived primarily as internal reviews to improve decision-making. Some of the growth of audits has been of this kind, intended to support rather than to discipline, and very different from ex post verifications which have much more the character of a policing role and for which the independence of the auditor is crucial. The extent to which audits are oriented towards verification is therefore variable and many commentators would wish to argue that value for money auditing plays an entirely different role.

But there are important linkages between the different contexts of audit. Forms of 'self-audit' rely upon bureaucratic procedures which can in principle be used for independent verification purposes, even in contexts such as medical audit.[15] Indeed, checklists and protocols for apparently internal purposes often derive their authority from their potential use for external verification. Formal documents can be used outside their original context and in ways unanticipated by those who may have designed them. In addition, the experience of other management areas suggests that even pre-decision reviews may have a ex post justificatory function.[16]

Second, that audit is not just a series of (rather uninteresting) technical practices. It must also be understood as an *idea*. It is usual, particularly in official documents and text books, to conceive of audit only in terms of its technical and operational qualities. While this image reinforces its reputation as a boring and parasitic practice, it disguises the importance of auditing as an idea. Audit has become central to ways of talking about administrative control. The extension of auditing into different settings, such as hospitals, schools, water companies, laboratories, and industrial processes, is more than a natural and self-evidently technical response to problems of governance and accountability. It has much to do with articulating values, with rationalising and reinforcing public images of control. The audit explosion is the explosion of an idea that is internal to the ways in which practitioners and policy makers make sense of what they are doing.[17]

Third, that the spread of audits and audit talk corresponds to a fundamental shift in patterns of governance in advanced industrial societies. As I have suggested above, the explosion of audit practices in new areas is, at least in the UK, not simply a quantitative intensification. It arises out of changing conceptions of administration and governance.[18] Accordingly, to understand this explosion we must dig deeper and look wider than preoccupations with technical and institutional issues. I wish to suggest that audit has emerged at the boundary between the older traditional control structures of industrial society and the demands of a society which is increasingly conscious of its production of risks, in fields ranging from the environment, to medicine and finance.[19] It is one of many features of a far-reaching transition in the dominant forms of administration and control, both in government and in business.

As such, audit is a way of reconciling contradictory forces: on the one hand the need to extend a traditional hierarchical command conception of control in order to maintain existing structures of authority; on the other the need to cope with the failure of this style of control, as it generates risks that are increasingly hard to specify and control.

Fourth, that the pervasive feature of the new wave of audits is that they work not on primary activities but rather on other systems of control. For example, recently proposed quality assurance mechanisms for higher education require audits of the quality assurance systems of higher education institutions.[20] This gives the audit a more remote assurance role than is often understood by the publics which they are intended to serve. It is in this sense that a gap between words and deed may exist -commonly referred to in financial audit contexts as an expectations gap. Audits are often not directly concerned with the quality of performance, whether environmental, educational or financial, but rather with the systems in place to govern quality. This 'policing of policing' distinguishes the audit explosion from an older tradition of engineering-based quality control and its statistically grounded methods.

Fifth, that audits do not contribute automatically to organisational transparency. Despite the fact that audit talk is driven by demands for greater transparency of organisational and individual action, the capacity of audit to deliver this is problematic. Often the extension of audits can make organisations more obscure, and the audit process itself remains publicly invisible despite the commitment to making organisations transparent. It may be that the audit explosion signifies a displacement of trust from one part of the economic system to another; from operatives to auditors.

Sixth, that audits have the remarkable capacity of being invulnerable to their own failure. In recent years the primary concern of public debate has been with financial audit. Often regarded as a model for other forms of audit, it has been the subject of extensive critical commentary, set off in large part by the recent demise of the Bank of Credit and Commerce International (BCCI) and the Maxwell empire. Rightly or wrongly, corporate collapse is always accompanied by scrutiny of the role of the auditors and, in some cases, litigation on the grounds that they have performed their task negligently.[21]

One of the surprising features of these experiences is that they tend not to call into question the role of audit itself. Instead, where audit has failed, the common response has been to call for more of it. Indeed, the great puzzle of financial audit is that it has never been a more powerful and influential model of administrative control than now, when many commentators talk of an auditing crisis.[22] Accordingly, I suggest that the audit explosion shares an important character with all kinds of policing: all have problematic criteria of success and are generally only publicly visible when they are seen to fail. But failure generally leads to a call for more policing and only rarely for a thorough analysis of why policing is failing.

Seventh, that audit is not passive but active. Not only does it shape the activities which it controls in critical ways but it represents a very particular conception of accountability. Far from being passive, audit actively constructs the contexts in which it operates. The most influential dimension of the audit explosion is the process by which environments are made auditable, structured to conform to the need to be monitored ex-post. Audits do not passively monitor auditee performance but shape the standards of this performance in crucial ways, and public conceptions of the very problems for which it is the solution.

Eighth, that, notwithstanding the dominance of audits there are other ways of achieving accountability.

These arguments are intended to demonstrate the institutional foothold that audit now has in the public imagination while raising serious questions about this impact. The central concern however is that the audit explosion has made it difficult to think of alternatives to itself. But any society or organisation can use very different models of control and accountability, which can be summarised in the following lists:

STYLE A	STYLE B
Quantitative	Qualitative
Single Measure	Multiple Measures
External Agencies	Internal Agencies
Long Distance Methods	Local Methods
Low Trust	High Trust
Discipline	Autonomy
Ex Post Control	Real Time Control
Private Experts	Public Dialogue

The audit explosion has involved an overwhelming priority for style A as the solution to any problem (although value for money auditing could be regarded as embodying both).[23] Quantified, simplified, ex-post forms of control by outsiders have increasingly displaced other types of control. As a result of its institutional power, and its power as an idea, proponents of alternative styles have found it hard to gain an audience.

This shift has brought a 'complex bundle of gains and losses'[24] and it is not the intention of this essay to suggest that there have been no gains at all from the growth of audit. However, these gains are likely to be most visible when used in conjunction with, rather than in opposition to, elements of control style B. One example of this is when medical audits help practitioners reflect on clinical methods and management as well as offering a mechanism for external evaluation. As in all things, the key is to achieve a balance and compromise. In this essay my purpose is to offer a diagnosis which may assist in restoring a balance that has been lost.

AUDITING AND THE SHAPING OF ACCOUNTABILITY

Auditing seems as natural and as necessary as policing. One may argue about its precise form, for example the balance between prevention and detection, but there is likely to be agreement that these things are done because of the way society is. Without them there would be more fraud, deception, waste, error and poor administration.

Specialised academic stories have formalised these intuitions about the need for audits: they will be demanded where there are relations of accountability between two parties together with a certain complexity or distance such that one, the 'principal', cannot easily and directly verify the activities of the other, the 'agent'.[25] In recent economic literature it is argued that it will be rational for the auditee to contract *voluntarily* to undergo an independent audit in order to make good offices visible. On this view audits are costly monitoring technologies which arise *naturally* under conditions where agents expose principals to 'moral hazards', because they may act against the principal's interests, and where there are 'information asymmetries', because they know more than the principals. Audit is therefore a risk reduction practice which inhibits the deviant actions of agents. At the extreme this implies that 'Four people performing a cooperative task, say loading trucks, find that the risk of any one of them slacking is such that they hire a fifth to monitor their work'.[26]

Audits are needed when accountability can no longer be sustained by informal relations of trust alone but must be formalised, made visible and subject to independent validation. This story can be told in relation to companies. When directors were generally regarded as trustworthy and shareholders were perceived as largely ignorant of business matters, financial audit was very limited. Despite being ruffled by the occasional scandal, confidence in the expertise and honesty of directors seemed a sufficient guarantee of financial accountability.

This consensus began to dissolve in the 1930s largely as a consequence of the famous Royal Mail case and subsequent reforms to company law.[27] Over time financial audit began to assume an ever more important regulatory function. The rise of the corporate economy, coupled with a statutory audit requirement, ensured its expanding influence and, by implication, that of its practitioners.

It has become commonplace to interpret these developments in terms of an erosion of trust. The financial audit arose because the relationship between management and increasingly distant providers of finance[28] was becoming problematic. The practical problems were also reflected - and reinforced - both by abstract economic theories of the corporation and by the organisation of Anglo-American capital markets.[29] It came to be accepted that actions could no longer be coordinated by trust and that instead independent 'outsiders' had to be used to restore that trust by providing ex post validations of auditee performance.

In banking and financial services auditors have in recent years assumed an increasingly visible regulatory role as informal control structures have been replaced. The demise of the Maxwell empire, and the regulatory responses which it has stimulated, can be interpreted as yet a further episode in the cycle of mistrust ensuring that despite public criticism, financial audits will become more intensive and more central in relation to questions of corporate governance.[30]

I want to suggest an alternative to this common view which sees audit as a response to problems of accountability that have originated elsewhere. Instead I will argue that audit has spread as much because of its power as an idea, and that contrary to the assumptions of the story of lost trust, its spread actually creates the very distrust it is meant to address.

It is important not to overstate this claim. It would certainly be far fetched to say that audit literally creates the pathologies for which it is the prescribed treatment, but I would not rule this out in particular cases. People may adapt their behaviour to reflect the fact that they are not trusted and thereby confirm that they should not be trusted. For example in higher education it has recently been suggested that academics have manipulated examination results to conceal matters from funding council quality assessors, something which they probably would not have done in the absence of an auditing process with funding implications.[31]

Moreover, in contrast to the popular image of audit as a derived and parasitic activity, audit shapes conceptions of accountability which favour audit as the solution.[32] 'Principals' and 'agent', may seem to be theoretical categories, abstractions from practical realities, but in different guises such as 'service provider' and 'customer', they have become common in official ways of talking about accountability.

But rather than solving the problem of trust, these models of accountability simply displace it.[33] If those engaged in everyday work are not trusted, then the locus of trust shifts to the experts involved in policing them, and to forms of documentary evidence or in management assurances about system integrity.[34] Ultimately there is a 'regress of mistrust' in which the performances of auditors and inspectors are themselves subjected to audit. Thus, Inland Revenue inspection has been subject to value for money audit as have the police force. A somewhat ironic parallel in finance has been the new regime for 'auditing the auditors' under the requirements of the Eighth European Community Directive on company law.

These examples show that the audit explosion is not simply a product of the rise of specific audit specialists, such as the 'Big Six' firms of accountants. It has much to do with the momentum of audit as an idea and as a system of knowledge.

Why then has the idea of audit, as a particular approach to accountability issues, become so prominent in recent years? How has the logic of audit become so widely generalised? The answer lies largely in transformations in the role of government and conceptions of governance.

AUDITING AND THE RETHINKING OF GOVERNMENT

A 'new public management' has taken shape in the last twenty years, influenced greatly by images of private sector administration. Public accountability has been reframed in relation to concepts such as goal definition, efficient resource allocation, financial performance and competition.[35] Of course, effectiveness of service delivery remains an ideal but it is less prominent and forms one, often subordinate, component of managerial language in the public sector.

This realignment of public management styles and objectives has a complex history which is beyond the scope of this analysis. However, for the purposes of this argument it is essential to understand that the reinvention of government[36] is informed by two opposite tendencies. On the one hand, there are centrifugal pressures for the decentralisation and devolution of services and for turning parts of government into enterprises, whether through full privatisation or partial 'enterprization'. Deregulatory initiatives and the investment of regulatory authority in 'private' control agencies, such as the Securities and Investments Board in the context of financial services, also reflect fundamental transformations in the style of government, away from direct provision and towards oversight and rule-setting.[37]

On the other hand, there are equally powerful pressures to retain control over functions that have been made autonomous. Financial oversight of Next Steps and other government agencies is one component. But as important is the intensive regulation of privatised utilities, and the strong, if delegated, regulation of financial markets in the name of consumer protection and market integrity.

These competing pressures, to devolve on the one hand and to control on the other, constitute a distinctive idea of government. Consistent with a liberal mission, the UK state is increasingly committed not to interfere or engage in service provision directly; it seeks to fulfil its role by more indirect supervisory means. In many cases the state has become regulator of last resort, operating indirectly through new forms of control (such as the independent regulator) which have the appearance of being apolitical. The great attraction of audit and accounting practices is that they appear to reconcile these centrifugal and centripetal forces better than the available alternatives.[38] The consequence is a displacement in the terms of government discourse, from service-specific values of teaching, care and so on to more abstract, financial and quantitative categories.

Why has this redesign of government happened? One plausible explanation is simply that the fiscal crisis of Western governments with generous welfare states has made much tighter financial disciplines necessary. While it is for future economic historians to judge, there is no doubt a great deal of truth in this story. However, it is also a little too lean and rational in its form. And it does not give us a feel for the particular forms which disciplines have taken.

For there have also been other sources of the audit explosion. One set of influences has been the growing preoccupations with quality assurance which can be traced in part to concerns about industrial competitiveness. Others include the breakdown of the consensus behind the welfare state, public grievances against experts and professionals, and the rise of human-made risks in nearly all areas of life.

In all these cases, the great attraction of the audit idea is its portability across such diverse contexts: public sector efficiency, corporate governance, environmental management systems and so on. The word symbolises a cluster of values: independent validation, efficiency, rationality, visibility almost irrespective of the mechanics of the practice and, in the final analysis, the promise of control. All of these apparent virtues have come together to make audit a central part of the 'reinvention of government'. But audit is not just an idea, it is not just a story of control. What gets done in its name matters and it is this that we must now consider.

AUDIT AS CONTROL OF CONTROL

One of the paradoxes of the audit explosion is that it does not correspond to more surveillance and more direct inspection.[39] Instead, audits generally act indirectly upon systems of control rather than directly upon first order activities.

As organisations have grown in scale and complexity, direct forms of inspection have become too expensive. Instead audits have become organised around internal systems of control. The paradigm example is the systems audit which is the conventional model for financial audits. Rather than examining large quantities of transactions, auditors focus on the control systems governing those transactions.[40] This is equally true of the work of the European Court of Auditors which, of necessity, relies heavily on the work of national agencies such as the UK's National Audit Office. Audit has thereby become the 'control of control',[41] where what is being assured is the quality of control systems rather than the quality of first order operations. In such a context accountability is discharged by demonstrating the existence of such systems of control, not by demonstrating good teaching, caring, manufacturing or banking.

Financial auditing texts promote this kind of systems audit as one of the higher stages in the evolution of the practice. But the truth is that they are rationalising a shift away from direct contact with practices which has been primarily driven by cost. The danger is that it is now more important to an organisation's legitimacy that it is seen to be audited than that there is any real substance to the audit. Even the fiercest critics have become caught up in this logic, as the public issue has become the independence of auditors rather than their competence or relevance.[42] What these critics ignore is that even with strong guarantees of independence, systems based audits can easily become a kind of ritual,[43] concerned with process rather than substance, and governed by a 'compliance mentality' which draws organisations away from their primary purposes.

But there is also another reason for the spread of systems audits beyond the economic unviability of real time inspection. As Day and Klein have argued in the context of the schools inspectorate, 'inspection... is about peer judgement by professionals reviewing the work of their fellow professionals'.[44] The justification for audit is that (at least for government) trust and valuation has moved away from the professionals, engineers or carers, so that even independent inspectors are not deemed trustworthy, because they are embedded within the profession. Instead only abstract systems of control can be deemed wholly independent.

This very abstraction from first order detail has greatly helped the explosion of audits in different fields. Detailed conceptions of quality may be very different if a supermarket is compared to a hospital. But the general principles of quality control systems for both can be made to look very similar, enabling one to compare them at an abstract level.

This is a recent development. In the nineteenth century, such financial audit guidance as existed was organised along industry-specific lines; the audit of railways was different from that of banks and so on. Over time this gave way to more abstract conceptions of the audit process despite the continuation of industry-specific guidance.[45] The systems audit represents another stage in this evolution; by abstracting from local organisational diversity it has enabled audit to assume the status of an almost irresistible cultural logic.

This mobility and diversity of application of audit is its great attraction; it can be invoked by marketeers and planners, entrepreneurs and regulators, consumers and producers, citizens and states. Indeed, as citizens' charters take hold audit will no doubt offer the prospect of realigning the relationship between patients and doctors, students and lecturers, passengers and transport operators.

But the institutional strength of audit also brings problems. Auditees develop creative strategies to cope with being audited. In many fields there is a sense that the tail of audit is increasingly wagging the dog of accountability and there are doubts about whether audits really empower the agents which they are intended to serve. It is to these questions that I now turn.

AUDITING AND THE IDEAL OF TRANSPARENCY

Accountability is so closely associated with ideas of transparency that the two concepts are often used interchangeably. Audits are usually justified as enhancing the transparency of individual and corporate actions to those parties who have an interest in the nature and effects of those actions. In other words, they are thought to shift power; from professionals to the public, from experts to stakeholders.

However, if we look more closely at the nature of this transparency and its democratising potential we soon find problems. How exactly does audit make things transparent? What are the mechanics of transparency?

To answer these questions we must distinguish two related issues: the transparency of the audit process and the transparency of audit findings.

The closure of the Bank of Credit and Commerce International in 1991 provides a good example. It stimulated considerable debate about the nature of the financial audit function in banks. However, the official report by Justice Bingham on the collapse did not concern itself with the audit *process*, preferring instead to deal with the requirement for auditors to report directly to bank supervisors.[46] Its justification was that questions of technical process are matters for the experts themselves. Whatever the merits of this view it means that the audit process, the mechanism by which organisations are made transparent, is not an object of public policy or open to scrutiny.

Most commentators would agree that this opacity of process, epitomised in the BCCI case, is at the heart of what is called the 'expectations gap' in financial auditing: the difference between how financial auditors are perceived (responsible for the detection of fraud) and how they see themselves (primarily responsible for forming a professional opinion on the financial statements).[47]

Over the years there has been much debate on this issue within the financial auditing profession. However, there are really only two possible solutions: either the users of audit opinions must be educated to have appropriate (lower?) expectations or the audit product must be brought into line with those expectations that do exist. In either case, the pressure is on those involved in financial audit to become more public about its objectives and process.

But throughout these debates on the audit 'expectations gap' there has been little appreciation that it can provide a useful service to both users and auditors. This is not as perverse an idea as it sounds, and it applies to all kinds of policing. Those doing the regulation, policing or auditing benefit from expectations which exceed what they can deliver, because these translate into higher fees and prestige. Meanwhile those in whose name the audits or policing is carried out benefit from a sense of assurance, even if this is not firmly grounded. Many would rather not know that their vulnerability is greater than it seems.

One could go further and suggest that the audit explosion has occurred at least in part because of, rather than despite, expectation gaps about the nature of audit. Its very ambiguity has helped it serve diverse needs,[48] and its opacity has helped its expanding role in government, serving the needs (and status) of the professionals involved, and comforting politicians and a wider public that things are under control. Audit can be likened to a shiny black box on the surface of which the aspirations of new regulatory programmes can be reflected and made possible. From this point of view, it is actually undesirable to look beneath the surface of audit practice into the box, to make the audit process more publicly transparent. In an important sense regulators do not want to know what auditing really is.

Another telling example of non-transparency is to be found in the field of environmental audits, where the general ambiguities of audit have been compounded by extensive concerns about what environmental audits really are. The widely accepted definition proposed by the International Chamber of Commerce requires that environmental audits are primarily a 'management tool'.[49] This managerial understanding of environmental audit has justified limiting their statutory status and their level of *public* disclosure. The justification for conceiving environmental audit in this way is to preserve it as a market based solution to problems of environmental risk.

The EC Environmental Management and Audit (EMA) scheme which was issued as a Regulation in 1992 is a voluntary scheme and requires auditors ('external verifiers') to validate a limited environmental statement. Whatever benefits these environmental audits may offer in terms of improved management systems, cost savings, legal compliance and so on, it is less clear how they contribute to the empowerment of external parties such as the public, local authorities, employees, shareholders or other firms. These uncertainties were shown all too clearly by the problems involved in compiling a public register of contaminated land in the UK, and the government's decision to withdraw proposals for such a register just before they were due to be introduced.

However, even extensive public disclosure in the name of transparency is an ambivalent phenomenon. Disclosure can have a pacifying effect on publics, can serve to convince them that something is or will be done by someone and can ultimately deter inquiry rather than encourage it. Disclosure can serve to amplify trust in the audit process rather than stimulate critical analysis of its results, since it often tends to shift trust towards new audit institutions, such as accreditation arrangements. The effect is to deter rather than invite inquiry about the auditee and the audit process. In other words trust in the fact that an audit is done displaces public preoccupations with what is done and what is discovered.

As we have already seen, the audit explosion is characterised less by an opening up of organisations and more by the reinvestment of trust in new bodies of audit expertise and its legitimation through such things as accreditation and monitoring systems. For accountants, this has taken the form of new disciplinary arrangements; for environmental auditors it has generated a politics of accreditation for external verifiers.[50] All are designed to build confidence in the practitioners of an audit function which remains hidden from view.[51]

The result is a paradox. The public image is that audits are conducted in the name of making visible the inner workings of organizations. Corporate financial audits are formally intended to serve the goal of shareholder control by linking the operations of corporate boardrooms to the decision-making calculus of distant financiers. Academic audits have as one of their goals the empowerment of a hitherto powerless student body. All promise external visibility of internal processes.[52] Yet audit is itself an increasingly private and invisible expert activity. The alternative may be simpler:

'So far, the emphasis of public policy has been to respond to complexity by setting up new institutions of accountability....this may, in turn, bring about excessive complexity in the machinery of accountability and at the same time create dead ends. So, why not concentrate less on formal links or institutions and engage more in a civic dialogue to recreate at least something of the high visibility and directness of the face to face accountability..'[53]

Alternatives of this kind, involving direct accountability and active interaction, have been almost wholly ignored by those who see audits as a universal panacea. But transparency alone does not empower, and paradoxically, may even serve to pacify and neutralise other possible forms of accountability, such as those based on answerability. At the extreme, audits which have become tightly interwoven in regulatory programmes can do more to promote obscurity than transparency.[54]

AUDITING AND REGULATORY FAILURE

The public image of audit is constantly threatened by 'real world' problems: the continuing visibility of 'healthy' companies which fail, the accumulation of ecological risks, the decline of educational standards, the misuse of public revenues and so on.[55]

However, in all these cases audit shares a characteristic with all policing activities: it is usually only at times of perceived failure that audits attract public attention. Successful auditing, even if this could be easily determined, is not very newsworthy. Indeed, one of the ironies of the audit explosion is that, despite being part of a culture that is much more concerned with institutional (and personal) performance, it is never easy to see how effective audits are. Crime rates may fall because of improved policing or because of demographic changes. Equally, corporate financial statements may be generally reliable because of good auditing or because of good company accounting policy.[56] In short, there is something profoundly elusive about the benefits of audit.[57]

The other side of the coin is that when things go wrong someone has to take the blame. As informal methods of regulation have given way to increasing formalisation, auditing has been periodically drawn into the blame allocation process. Legal judgments are the most important part of that process but there are many others, not least of which is critical press comment. Regulators often also blame each other. The fraud related collapse of Barlow Clowes, the Levitt Group and others attracted considerable adverse press comment but there was also evidence of pressures between auditors and regulators with the latter often seeking to blame and reform the former.[58]

Failures tend to lead to a combination of complex negotiations to allocate blame together with reforms of the audit process. Thus, in the case of the collapse of BCCI and its aftermath the response has focused in part on the blameworthiness of auditors Price Waterhouse, and new codified guidance to auditors is to be produced; auditors will soon have a statutory duty to report to regulators on certain matters rather than, as prior to BCCI, a right to do so.[59]

But amongst these various battles to pass the buck, there is a striking general trend; that audit almost always becomes more explicitly codified in the wake of processes of blame allocation. In the wake of scandals and frauds, audit failure is usually located as a *particular* problem of fraudulent management or credulous auditors and is addressed by extensive *codification* of new official audit guidance. The principle seems to be that the general efficacy of audit must be preserved even if the reputation of particular practitioners is not.

These are complex processes but the tendencies are clear. Successive sequences of failure involve the use of audits as a restorer of comfort, each time in a more intensive form, and each time apparently better immunised against failure, since every failure is particular and every solution general. And in all this there is a good deal of cosmetics. Indeed, technically detailed realignments of audit practice sometimes resemble the elaboration of epicycles to preserve Ptolomaic cosmology, an impressive effect of form rather than content.

Similar doubts apply to the validity of environmental audit as a management tool which functions to reconcile commercial advantage and the production of goods to environmental concerns about the production of bads.[60] This reconciliation is epitomised by the concept of BATNEEC, Best Available Technology Not Entailing Excessive Cost. So far, environmental auditing does not yet have its BCCI or Maxwell and so we cannot point to a regulatory failure. However, we should be wary, since environmental audit may come to assume an institutional importance similar to that of financial audit and is already making alternatives to itself unthinkable.

We should be sceptical above all because audit embodies a not always justifiable optimism about the possibility of achieving control over processes which have become ever more complex, such as European Union fraud, industrial pollution and so on. Rather than solving problems, it may also insulate us from that complexity, despite the occasional scandal, in order to preserve faith in its efficacy. That faith depends in turn on matters of organization or process always being auditable. It is to this dimension of the audit explosion that I now turn.

MAKING THINGS AUDITABLE

The public image of auditing as a dull but worthy practice implies that it is neutral. Official views emphasise the collection of evidence of an appropriate quality and quantity.[61] If unambiguous standards of auditee performance can be established, then audit simply verifies compliance with such standards. Where there is deviation from standards then auditors report and advise. From this point of view, the standards of auditee performance are independent of the audit process.

Yet the opposite is often the case. Audits do as much to construct definitions of quality and performance as to monitor them. For example, financial accountability demands financial audit as a control over the 'quality' of the accounts provided by the auditee and the auditor achieves this by the periodic and independent ex post inspection of books, records and control systems. However, most financial auditors would admit, and take some pride in, their often decisive influence on the standards of performance to which the auditee is subjected. They are far from being neutral relays in an exogenously given accountability system. Not only do these standards of financially conceived performance make the accountability of corporations visible in highly specific ways; they also constitute a 'financial rationality' which has been influential in recent transformations in public sector audit practice.

Public sector audits officially enable government bodies, via the operations of the UK NAO and the Audit Commission, to observe themselves critically and objectively in the service of initiatives in public financial management and policy accountability. There has been much debate about the policy neutrality of Value For Money (VFM) auditing and the role of the NAO more generally, and it is becoming widely recognised that VFM audit, which lies at the heart of these changes, is much more than a monitoring 'technique'. It is intended both to evaluate and to shape the performance of the auditee in three dimensions: economy, efficiency and effectiveness.

However, it is well known that in many service sectors the notion of effectiveness is not easily calibrated and requires a range of financial and non-financial measures. It has been suggested that VFM prioritises that which can be measured and audited in economic terms - efficiency and economy - over that which is more ambiguous and local - effectiveness.[62]

Performance in the sense of effectiveness is difficult to assess where practitioners are unaccustomed to thinking in such terms. For example, nurses, policemen and women, prison officers, research workers and others, have traditionally used highly localised standards of quality control. In all these cases, too, concepts of success and failure are problematic: rising levels of ill-health, crime and prison disorder have many causes and cannot simply be regarded as 'failures' of the service in question. For all its proclaimed sensitivity towards context, VFM demands that effectiveness be quantifiable. It does this by standardising measures of effectiveness (on the one hand) and/or by reducing effectiveness to standardisable measures of economy and efficiency. Either way, there is a necessary drift towards 'managing by numbers' which enables a drift towards centralised forms of control and the displacement of concerns about good policy by concerns about good management.[63]

Where the measurement and attribution of outputs from a service are ambiguous, or the preserve of the service expert, there is a tendency to concentrate upon inputs. For example, in the case of child care it may be that social workers themselves are unable to agree about whether fostering or residential care is most effective in nurturing the balanced development of children. In this case, it is natural to focus on unambiguous measures of input, primarily cost. It follows that efficiency in this context may come to be seen in terms of cost saving for existing levels of service provision rather than an improved relationship between inputs and outputs, which in industrial contexts represents productivity.[64] In this way, like other forms of audit, VFM involves a displacement from first order experts, such as teachers, social workers, police and so on to second order experts, such as accountants and managers.

These displacements do not necessarily reflect public distributions of trust. Indeed it is an irony that audits of this kind bring a shift from professions the public trusts more -such as doctors, police and teachers, to a profession the public trusts less (the accountants) at the instigation of a profession the public trusts least (the politicians).

Undoubtedly, there are benefits from disturbing closed professional cultures; local forms of peer review may simply foster a tyranny of expertise. VFM may be genuinely democratising, opening up performance to wider scrutiny. Measures of economy, efficiency and effectiveness may be arbitrary but if they are widely accepted they may also be impartial and public.[65] However, against the possible benefits of a new impersonal objectivity in public service must be weighed the transformations in the service itself. It is a difficult balance.

The concept of VFM has also become increasingly linked to that of quality despite their different institutional origins. Recent initiatives in academic audit for both teaching and research provide another interesting example of the complex logic of audit process because here too there is currently widespread debate about what constitutes quality.[66] There has been widespread concern that the Research Assessment Exercises conducted by the higher education authorities in the UK have contributed to a climate in which quantity takes precendence over the quality of publications[67] because of the mechanisms of research output measurement which enable an audit of research performance to be conducted. The significant economic consequences of such audits inevitably generate new incentive structures for researchers. The problem is not that review and assessment methods are wrong per se but that the very technologies of audit may paradoxically achieve the opposite of their intended effect.

One other element of this debate is the role of users - specifically in this case the weight to be attached to student questionnaires as measures of teaching quality. Many lecturers favour questionnaires and were using them as a form of self-audit prior to the recent initiatives. Others are opposed on principle. Whatever the intrinsic merits, questionnaires make teaching 'auditable', and thus easier to regulate in the name of quality.[68] In other words what is at stake here are not only the declared objectives, the improvement of teaching quality, but also a style of control over teaching. The ideal of 'auditability' gives commitments to quality and effectiveness operational meaning.

For verificatory activity always requires that there is something verifiable. In many instances, these types of information are required by legislation; for example, company law requirements for financial reporting and the maintenance of proper books and records, or other arrangements such as the pronouncements of organisations such as the British Standards Institute (BSI) and the Higher Education Funding Council which emphasise the role of control systems.[69]

It was noted in the introduction that audit is generally a form of control of control. What is subject to inspection is the auditee's own system for self monitoring rather than the real practices of the auditee.[70] What is audited is whether there is a system which embodies standards and the standards of performance themselves are shaped by the need to be auditable. In this way, the existence of a system is more significant for audit purposes than what the system is; audit becomes a formal 'loop' by which the system observes itself.[71] While there is a sense in which this immunises the auditee from the audit process, the necessity of having an 'auditable system' nevertheless impacts upon real time practices and has obvious resource implications for auditees. Auditable systems require subjects to represent themselves primarily as auditees. Undoubtedly, new games will emerge around these systems-driven audit processes. Forms of 'non-compliance compliance' and creative strategies of submitting to audit processes will frustrate the mission of audit.[72] At the same time organisations may be encumbered with structures of auditability embodying performance measures which increasingly do not correspond to the first order reality of practitioners' work.

The construction of auditability around auditable systems is perhaps most evident in the British Standards Institute initiatives on quality assurance (BS5750) and environmental management systems (BS7750). Both standards, which are highly abstract as compared to other BSI standards, emphasise the development of management control systems. The standards are the core of an accreditation process which has become a new product and is sold to companies who wish to gain a marketing advantage from being seen to comply.

These BSI standards have focused managerial attention in many beneficial directions but it is also true that their value as products resides to a great extent in their promise of auditability qua accreditability.

The critical question is whether the ideal of auditability implicit in these initiatives may in fact eclipse the development of first order standards themselves. The assurance process may simply become too important. BS7750 has been developed with a view to requiring companies to articulate their own benchmarks of environmental performance against which they can improve in subsequent years. Hence, BS7750 articulates the structure of an environmental management system but not the standards of performance themselves. While this is likely to concentrate managerial energies in positive directions there are also dangers as audit begins to take on a life of its own increasingly decoupled from the processes and events which it is intended to address.

The most recent instance of this tendency is the draft guidance for external verifiers under the EMA scheme,[73] which is symptomatic of the way auditing creates webs of increasingly dense procedure and compliance checklist of suitably elaborate detail.[74] The ideal checklist reflects the relevant performance of the auditee and ensures the completeness and visibility of audit work. The checklist determines the relevant facts about the auditee and insulates the particular auditor from needing to worry about the background to the list, as well as providing him or her with a defence against critics, especially in a court of law.

But what should be the knowledge basis of audit? Some would say that legal knowledge is crucial. However, the auditor has always been burdened with the need to understand the regulatory environment of the audited entity. In my view the key to auditing is the 'inferential logic' (or lack of it) which enables an auditor to form conclusions about the whole on the basis of examining and testing some of its parts. At various periods in its history, financial audit practice has attempted to establish linkages between a non-inferential procedural knowledge base and 'higher', abstract bodies of inferential knowledge.[75] However, the latter have been invoked as much to confer scientific credibility upon the practice as to provide instrumental guidance. Hopes were expressed that statistical sampling could place auditing on a scientific footing and the importance of sampling technologies to a scientific image of audit cannot be underestimated. Indeed, the symbolic importance of statistical sampling is relatively unaffected by its actual applications. As a way of talking, writing and justifying, sampling makes possible rational representations of the audit process, and thereby of the auditee.[76]

The general point is that the system of auditing knowledge is increasingly self-referential. It models organisations for its own purposes and impacts to varying degrees upon their first-order operations. Ironically, one area where this is particularly apparent is in the context of the regulatory arrangements for financial auditors in the UK which have come about as a consequence of the EC Eighth Directive on Company Law. This imposed new requirements for the regulation of financial auditors, including that they should be licensed and subjected to compliance visits by monitors.[77] These compliance audits are decoupled from underlying organisational processes but nevertheless force the auditee to take on some of the shapes required by the audit process, if only because resources are being spent on compliance.[78]

The policy question is whether it has all gone too far. Are auditing mechanisms of control themselves out of control? Is there a price to be paid for a logic of auditability? Are there real benefits to service quality and effectiveness which override the local doubts of threatened practitioners? Or is the language of quality and VFM an elaborate rhetoric for cost reduction in the face of a public sector borrowing crisis? There is no doubt that VFM has been instrumental in the reorganization of public life around audit and accounting processes which make organisations 'selectively visible'.[79] And there can be no doubt about the momentum which quality assurance initiatives now have.

In a real sense power has shifted from social workers, doctors, and other public sector workers towards auditors and quality insurance inspectors because the latter increasingly control the terms of public discourse. Moreover their power is such that there is now almost no way that reservations about audit can be articulated without appearing to defend privileges and secrecy.

However, the logic of auditability is far from being entirely monolithic and public concerns about too much reviewing, about preoccupations with systems rather than performance and about the cost of audit in relation to its claimed efficacy are becoming more apparent. So what is to be done?

BEYOND AUDIT

The analysis developed above is intended to be critical but without being wholly dismissive. It does not point to a conspiracy of the vested interests of accounting practitioners since the audit explosion is visible in areas where they have little influence. Rather I have attempted to supply a diagnosis of the position in which we find ourselves. Before we can make prescriptions about how audit practices may be re-designed, we need to understand the economic and political conditions under which a practice,which might ordinarily be regarded as supplementary to other forms of administration, has become so central.

We seem to have lost an ability to be publicly sceptical about the fashion for audit and quality assurance; they appear as 'natural' solutions to the problems we face. And yet, just as other fashions have come and gone as the basis for management thinking, the audit explosion is also likely to be a passing phase.

The seeds of a change may be there. There is certainly dissatisfaction with the primacy of audit which is becoming more vocal. Firstly, the cost of audit in relation to its claimed benefits, particular in the fields of financial audit and quality assurance arrangements, is being questioned in the light of its potential impact upon competitiveness. Secondly, there may be difficulties with the public legitimacy of accountants, particularly in the public sector. A recent survey of public opinion suggests, as noted earlier, that accountants are less unpopular than politicians but much less popular than the police, teachers and doctors.[80] Thirdly, there are concerns about organisational governance and the efficacy of audit arrangements in relation to them. In other words, the syndromes of regulatory failure may not always reaffirm the mission of audit; for example, some would now argue that capital market stability might be better served by increasing the internal representation of institutional stakeholders rather than by reliance on external forms of measurement and oversight.

But these grievances do not yet form part of an institutionally acceptable language. The first difficulty in creating such a language is that we need to generate a scepticism about our current preoccupations with ideals of 'performance' and 'quality' and the technologies through which they are made operational while recognising that such a scepticism has dangers; namely that it risks ignoring the benefits of audit and providing an apologia for outmoded forms of expert privilege, insulating actors from all forms of responsibility and thereby threatening accountability itself.

The second difficulty is that if policy recommendations are to be constructed on the back of the diagnosis which I have offered then they will need to find their primary conceptual resources in some very unfashionable areas. For example, concepts of trust and autonomy will need to be partially rehabilitated into managerial languages in some way. In the mid 1990s we have reached a position where, in the pursuit of performance measurement, anxieties have been fuelled that threaten to destroy the commitment of individuals to their organisations to such an extent that this may undermine performance. Insecurity among senior executives calls into question the very idea of 'organisational loyalty'.[81] The audit explosion is not the only culprit here but it is one of a range of administrative instruments which threaten to be as much part of the problem as of the cure.

It should be clear that the policy issue is not simply a question of reducing the quantity of auditing. It is rather to design organisations in such a way that they better manage themselves and their relationships to outsiders so that audit is not automatically seen as a 'natural' solution. If one dominant institutional logic is to be replaced, then new ones must fill what would otherwise be a vacuum. My proposals can only be suggestive but if audit is as much a norm as a technical practice then it follows that one needs new vocabularies as well as new practices.

Firstly, a new respect for local specificity needs to be generated and, by the same token, a suspicion of control instruments which standardise from a distance. This suspicion already exists but it requires institutional mechanisms to give it voice and to make public the potential of audit practices to create systems which serve the audit process and little else. We may need to give up certain myths of long distance regulation.[82]

Accordingly, the concept of accountability needs to be both loosened and tightened. It needs to be loosened as regards the levels of ritualistic detail through which auditability is conducted by remote agencies of control. The benefits of these highly elaborated audit procedures are increasingly out of line with the burden of costs which they impose upon the auditee.[83] However, this loosening must also be supplemented by performance concepts which seek to restore, at the extreme, face to face forms of peer group accountability and structures which cut through layers of process and make organisational dialogue possible. Some might see this as an appeal to self-regulation and the restoration of expert privilege but it is more an argument that corporate community is a necessary precondition for corporate governance. The tension between consensus and discipline is a constant difficulty as recent criticism about the style of HEFC academic audit reports indicates.[84]

Whereas recent initiatives in corporate governance seem to have magnified the importance of audit, it must be possible to conceive of governance outside this framework. For this we will need to take seriously new institutional spaces in which stakeholders of every variety can assert their claims as 'principals'. Rather than placing faith in audit committee mechanisms, a greater variety of possibilities for representative forums needs to be considered. Public discussion about the benefits of the Cadbury proposals has gravitated towards the costs and benefits of non-executive directors; the efficacy of committees of this kind is more or less assumed.[85]

Secondly, we need to generate a healthy scepticism about official modes of disclosure and audit and to experiment with non-(financial) accounting and non-audit based methods linking stakeholders and enterprises. Again, new languages are needed. Performance measurement will need to be supplemented by qualitative concepts such as facilitation. In addition we will require new ways of defining the boundaries of organisations since audit arises from the externalisation of insiders (more traditionally described as the separation of ownership from control) and the self-fulfilling image of the corporation as a network of contracts.

Where audit and the forms of disclosure which arise out of it reinforce the externality of outside stakeholders, we may need organisational innovations through which they can be brought back in through rights of access and inquiry. Accounting and auditing conceptions of the 'user' of financial statements are generally very abstract. While accounting and information system re-design will continue to play an important role, so too may forms of organisational participation for real as opposed to mythical users of financial information. Whereas audited disclosure tends to deter inquiry and encourage trust in the audit process, other mechanisms may be capable of encouraging and sustaining inquiry. Forms of internalisation of stakeholders may also be information-efficient to the extent that formal audit and accounting would become redundant. In addition, institutionalised avenues for whistleblowing, a practice from which the Inland Revenue has benefited, could provide another alternative to the audit model.[86]

In the light of these suggestions the ambivalence of Citizens' Charters must be noted. Such charters embody a mixture of rights to know and rights to choose. However, it is likely that the right to choose will not have much substance if the choices in question run counter to the need to curtail public expenditure. If so, the operational weight of citizens' charters will fall upon the right to know or, in other words, the transparency of service organisations. In this respect it must be asked whether they really herald a new era of popular governance driven by participation and dialogue or whether they will effectively become an 'Auditors' Charter', a symptom of the failure of democracy and empowerment rather than its cure.[87]

In addition, there needs to be greater sensitivity to the manner in which instruments of verification can transform the contexts in which they are applied and can bias accountability in unintended directions. Decisions need to be taken about whether this is desirable or not and, in place of faith, some empirical knowledge needs to be acquired about the behavioural effects of auditing in different fields. For the audit explosion has been driven less by an empirically grounded understanding of the productive benefits of audit and more by a pervasive belief, almost ideological in form, in the need for the discipline which it provides. It is ironic that in many instances audit practices are themselves insulated from the market forces and ideals of deregulation which they serve.

In the end, looking beyond audit requires that we also rethink what it is that makes organisations work. Western fascination for Japanese organisational structures seems to have been unable to affect the audit mentality.[88] Japanese structures depend much more on 'style B' types of control: horizontal rather than vertical, trust-creating, qualitative rather than quantitative.

Like them, we would benefit from having less respect for abstract forms of portable knowledge and more respect for non-standard and tacit kinds of knowledge which are complex and close to their products. Here I would make a personal plea on behalf of the complexity of university teaching. The tide of consumer enfranchisement may empower students in one sense but it may also impoverish them in the longer run by cultivating an aversion to difficulty, ambiguity and critique unless it is carefully managed. Courses will increasingly be designed primarily with student evaluations and other audits in mind such that teachers will avoid risk and therefore innovation. Without wishing to invoke a mythic golden age, an important relationship between teachers and students may nevertheless be damaged.[89]

In looking beyond audit an entire regulatory apparatus will need to be redesigned with the question, 'What are organisations for?' firmly in its sights. The interim report of the RSA inquiry into 'Tomorrow's Company' points to the need for an 'inclusive approach' which is localist in regulatory spirit and clearly has implications for auditing.[90] If we end up using more of the Style A forms of audit described in section 1, they will need to be light and modest compliance exercises which do not generate more expectations than they merit and whose benefits can be clearly articulated. Although this will undoubtedly challenge existing structures of professional status, we will not be sending the nation's brightest and best to work in an abstract 'economy of compliance'. Instead we will be placing them closer to the productive processes - in services, manufacturing and the public sector - in all their diversity. In this way we will surely be in a better position to create quality rather than just to police it.

SUMMARY

1.   There has been an explosion of audits in many different fields: medicine, science, education, technology, environment, intellectual property to name but a few. Audit has assumed the status of an all purpose solution to problems of administrative control. Despite concerns about its costs, the benefits of audit are assumed by its proponents rather than proven. Even though the efficacy of financial audit is currently being doubted as never before, particularly in the wake of corporate scandals, auditing remains powerful. Indeed, alternative mechanisms of long-distance control have become almost unthinkable.

Audit is an emerging principle of social organization which may be reaching its most extreme form in late twentieth-century Britain. It is as important as an ideal - a set of ideas or logics - as a practice. Many audit practices have grown because of changes in public sector management and newly prominent ideals of quality, governance and accountability. And yet paradoxically, while audit technologies have contributed to managerial concerns about 'performance', the performance of audit itself is far from being unambiguous and free from public dispute. But the spread of audits constitutes a major shift in power: from the public to the professional, and from teachers, engineers and managers to overseers.

2.   Audits are not simply answers to problems of accountability. They also shape the contexts in which they are demanded in important ways. Submission to audit has become such a benchmark of institutional legitimacy that resistance and complaint look like attempts to preserve abuses of privilege and secrecy. The audit explosion has its origins in very recent transformations of government which have sought to devolve many of its functions while retaining regulatory oversight.

3.   Audit is linked to ideals of organisational transparency and accountability. Yet audits are themselves often very specialised and opaque to a wider public. Audits may provide comfort to stakeholders who are remote from day to day practices but, in doing so, they often deter substantive inquiry which would empower stakeholders. Audit arrangements can bring an end to dialogue inside and outside organisations, rather than helping it. In so far as audit is directed at evoking good feelings about organisational practices it may also become a new form of image management rather than a basis for substantive analysis. In this sense, the fact of audit is becoming more important than the how of audit.

4.   Audits are usually publicly visible when they fail. Their benefits are often ambivalent and a source of controversy. Audit reconstitutes itself in a syndrome of regulatory failure: it emerges from crises institutionally secure despite processes of blame allocation within the regulatory world. Problems are defined as particular, while general solutions are usually offered. With each crisis, audits become more formalised and intensive.

5.   Audits are not passive practices but strongly influence the environments in which they operate. Instead of involving direct observation, audit is largely an indirect form of 'control of control' which acts on systems whose role is to provide observable traces. In a number of areas this results in a preoccupation with the auditable process rather than the substance of activities. This in turn burdens the auditee with the need to invest in mechanisms of compliance, a fact which has produced a consistent stream of complaint. Concepts of performance and quality are in danger of being defined largely in terms of conformity to auditable process. Indeed, the construction of auditable environments has necessitated record-keeping demands which only serve the audit process.

6. Auditing is a peculiar form of alchemy which, in making auditees auditable, produces regulatory comfort. It is conservative not in the sense of a conspiracy of vested interests, but in the sense of being a system of knowledge which filters and appropriates the unforeseen. In the process of constructing subjects as responsible auditees local structures of trust are displaced and potentially distorted. Any reduction in audit intensity, and the possibility of forms of organisation in which groups and individuals are given autonomy, is literally unthinkable without a new institutional language which does not so much reject audit as assign it to its proper place.

In looking beyond audit we shall need to recognise that a certain style of accountability, which values independent scrutiny, is one value among others. Audit displaces trust from first-order to second-order verificatory activities. We may need to rehabilitate trust at the level of first-order performance, change the organisational conditions under which audit appears to emerge naturally and even give up on the ritualistic details in which accountability is discharged by audit. In doing so we need to reposition audit as a local and facilitative practice, rather than one that is remote and disciplinary, so as to enable rather than inhibit public dialogue. External forms of audit will need to be more modestly conceived. This will require a broad shift in control philosophy: from long distance, low trust, quantitative, disciplinary and ex-post forms of verification by private experts to local, high trust, qualitative, enabling, real time forms of dialogue with peers. In this way we may eventually be in a position to devote more resources to creating quality rather than just to policing it.

NOTES

1 It has also been brought to my attention that the terms 'audit' and 'auditor' have for many years played a central role in the ideas of the Church of Scientology.

2 This essay is based in part upon, 'The Audit Society' forthcoming in Anthony Hopwood and Peter Miller (Eds) *Accounting as Social and Institutional Practice*, Cambridge University Press, Cambridge, 1994.

3 See Carol Jones, 'Auditing Criminal Justice' *British Journal of Criminology* Vol 33, No.2, Spring 1993, pp.187-202.

4 See, *Working for patients*, HMSO London, 1989.

5 The HEFC has advertised for a number of posts in early 1994, including quality auditors on a part-time basis. The job description is interesting because management experience in relation to education is preferred but is not regarded as essential.

6 See 'UK prospects in the booming global environmental market' *ENDS Report* 212 (September 1992).

7 See 'Environmental consultants ride out recession' *ENDS Report* 213 (October 1992).

8 See, 'NACCB to be accreditation body for BS7750 and EC Eco-Audit' *ENDS Report* (November 1993) pp.36-7.

9 See, *University Statistics 1991-92*, HMSO, 1993, pp.64-5.
10 For evidence of the burden on small companies, see 'Unloved expense' *The Financial Times* February 2 1993.

11 Of nearly 13,5000 charities registered with the Charity Commission, only 11% submitted accounts to them in the early 1990s. See 'Act of charity brings audit day of reckoning' *The Financial Times* 19 November 1992.

12 A new journal entitled *Accountability in Research: Policies and Quality Assurance*, was launched in 1989.

13 See, for example the white paper, *Realising our potential: A strategy for science, engineering and technology*, HMSO, London 1993. The new public management of science is discussed in Brad Sherman, 'Governing Science: Patents and Public Sector Research', *Science in Context*, forthcoming, Vol 7, no. 3, 1994.

14 In this sense I am drawn to the claim that 'The canon of exhaustion of evidence is a peculiar one; it seems tied to an increasing miniaturization of focus, so that the more we "know" about a subject, the more details we know. Anaesthetization of the intellect is the inevitable product of this form of proof..' Richard Sennett, *The Fall of Public Man*, Faber and Faber, London 1986, p.43.

15 See Adrian Gain and Jonathan Rosenhead, 'Problem Structuring for Medical Quality Assurance' *LSE Working Papers in Operational Research* (November 1993). This empirical study reports on various ways to generate consensus and shared objectives around the audit process. However, in the design of audit arrangements the tensions between clinical and managerial resource-based judgements proved the most intractable, with clinicians having considerable anxiety about the coopting of audit processes for disciplinary purposes.

16 For an exploration of this see Nils Brunsson, 'Ideas and Action: Justification and Hypocrisy as Alternatives to Control', *Accounting, Organizations and Society* (1993) Vol 18, No. 6, pp.489-506.

17 These comments draw heavily from Stanley Cohen, *Visions of Social Control*, Polity Press, Cambridge 1985, pp.155-160.

18 It would be easy to regard the audit explosion as extending rationalisation in Weber's sense. Certainly it creates its own bureaucratic machinery and can be regarded as a form of rationalisation. But its instrumentality is problematic and often obscure. One therefore has a puzzle which escapes Weber's framework: widespread investment in a practice with ambiguous functional credentials.

19 See Ulrich Beck, *Risk Society* Sage, London, 1992.

20 See 'The Special Intelligence Agency' *The Times Higher* September 24 1993 pp.16-17. This article contains a cartoon which epitomises the essential structure of the audit society. It depicts a large quality assurance inspector checking over the shoulder of another smaller official who is in turn checking the work of another even smaller individual whose identity as lecturer or student is not made clear. The quality assurance inspector is remote from the first order activity. His or her role is that of control of control.

21 Critics, such as the Labour Party MP Austen Mitchell, regard independence as the underlying problem. They argue that financial auditors are too close to the interests of management who control their remuneration. Accordingly the objectivity of auditors is systematically impaired and can only be improved by institutional change. These critics suggest that a new body, such as a general audit council, could provide the necessary oversight and effective discipline. Others see the problem in terms of the expectations which audit creates among consumers and the 'gap' between them and auditors' own conception of their mission. Initial responses to this problem have been conceived in terms of educating consumers of audit services to have the 'correct' expectations. Now there is an, albeit cautious, mood for a different response - to bring the audit product into line with these expectations (See Christopher Humphrey, Peter Moizer and Stuart Turley, *The Audit Expectations Gap in the United Kingdom* Institute of Chartered Accountants in England and Wales, London 1991). While practitioners can be precise about the costs of audit, its benefits in terms of providing assurance to other parties about the quality of financial statements have consistently defied precision, despite attempts to integrate statistical techniques into audit programmes.

22 This crisis has different faces. Firstly, financial audit practitioners are facing a mature market experiencing competition with a vengeance. Secondly, they are also facing a growth in litigation (not yet evident in other fields of auditing) which is increasing the risk they face (See 'Auditors turn cold as legal claims hot up' *The Financial Times* October 11 1993). Thirdly, they are experiencing an erosion of reputation as the consuming public begins to doubt the value of this statutory product. Under these circumstances it is to be expected that audit firms would seek to diversify into markets for other services, including audits in other areas.

23 I would not necessarily concede that 'democracy' and 'communications audits' are exceptions to my claim since the mechanics of audit, even if designed with style B in mind, has the potential to drift towards style A. See David Beetham, *Auditing Democracy in Britain*, Charter 88 Trust Publications, London 1992; A. Booth, *Communications Audit: A Guide for Managers*, Gower, London 1988.

24 See 'Auditing the Accountants' *The Political Quarterly* Vol. 64, No.3, 1993, p.270.
25 David Flint, *Philosophy and Principles of Auditing*, Macmillan Education, London 1988. Flint argues that the 'primary condition for an audit is that there is a relationship of accountability or a situation of public accountability' (p.23). On this view accountability relations are *logically prior* to audits.

26 See Charles Perrow, 'Economic Theories of Organization' in Sharon Zukin and Paul DiMaggio (eds) *Structures of Capital: The Social Organization of the Economy*, Cambridge University Press, Cambridge 1990, p.123. Perrow is generally critical of the abstraction from institutional context which sustains this form of analysis. He also argues that the working assumptions of agency theory reflect a capitalist form of production which 'started because four workers could not trust each other' (p.123). Indeed, one of the dangers of agency theory for Perrow is that people increasingly think in its terms. Perrow also suggests that the monitor becomes dominant in relation to the four

workers. This suggests that the performance of those who are monitored must be registered in such a way as to make monitoring possible. I develop this theme further in section 7 of the introduction.

27 See Dick Edwards, *A History of Financial Accounting*, London: Routledge, 1989, chapter 12.

28 Despite the fact that traditional histories of financial audit describe its emergence in terms of the separation of ownership (principals) and control (agents), the demands of capital markets and the varied forms of regulating the enterprise, its precise role has never been uncontested. Questions of auditor liability and shifting public expectations, usually in the light of perceived audit failure, have been more or less continuous pressures for modification and change. In the UK, there has recently been renewed concern with the manner in which financial audit serves shareholders who are remote from the audit process. The Cadbury Report on Corporate Governance can be interpreted in part as an attempt to revitalise the accountability relationship upon which financial audit depends by devising mechanisms to make shareholders internally visible. In this way, the category of 'principal' must be constantly reinforced if it is not to become merely formal.

29 See Michael Jensen and William Meckling, 'Theory of the Firm: Managerial Behaviour, Agency Costs and Ownership Structure' *Journal of Financial Economics*, 1976, pp.305-60. This famous essay has influenced not only generations of economic theorists but has also filtered into organisational thinking. Economics has this distinctive property that its theories can become true by virtue of the world changing to conform to the theory. Assumptions which are initially abstract from the world often become the basis for changing it.

30 See Coopers & Lybrand, *Executive Briefing: Corporate Governance and the Role of the Auditor*, June 1992, for evidence that financial auditors are hesitant about this extension of their role and responsibilities. See also 'Pieces of Cadbury still await consumption' *The Financial Times* February 3 1994.

31 See 'The parts assessors can't reach' *The Times Higher Educational Supplement*, February 4 1994.

32 I have argued that this is particularly the case in emerging contexts of auditing. See Michael Power, 'Auditing and Environmental Expertise: Between Protest and Professionalisation', *Accounting, Auditing and Accountability Journal*, 1991, Vol.4, No.3, pp.37-62. In the context of environmental audit practices, the audit is developing prior to the institutionalisation of an accountability framework. Audit is shaping this framework in distinctive ways by, for example, emphasising the role of audit as a 'management tool'. In this way the negotiability of the category of principal is preempted and normalised. Despite claims that the relevant 'principals' are communities, future generations or even nature as such, environmental audit has emerged as a practice with a strong managerial flavour. This contrasts with earlier forms of 'social' audit which sought to contest and protest against corporate environmental effects.

33 See Peter Armstrong, 'Contradiction and Social Dynamics in the Capitalist Agency Relationship' *Accounting, Organizations and Society*, 1991, pp.1-25. Like Perrow, Armstrong suggests that the 'visualisation of organisations as systems of contracts' is central to the cogency of agency theories of organisation. However, contracts never substitute entirely for trust but only displace it. Hence the reliance on monitors such as auditors to restore trust is a potential regress. Armstrong argues that this displacement of trust is primarily responsible for the rise of the monitor at the expense of operational management in British Industry. Once set in motion, 'An accounting managerial culture creates both a supply and a demand for additional accounting functions which therefore tend to expand...' (p.19).

34 The Auditing Practices Board is currently revising the structure of auditing standards. These three areas will be covered by three new Statements of Audit Standard (SAS): 300 'Audit Risk Assessment'; 440 'Management Representations'; 520 'Using the work of an expert'.

35 See Christopher Hood, 'A Public Management for All Seasons', *Public Administration*, 1991, pp.3-19. These changes cannot simply be laid at the door of Thatcherism since they have parallels throughout developed economies. Certainly there are supply side peculiarities in the UK and the role of the large accountancy firms is one factor. As Christopher Lasch suggests, professions invent many of the needs which they claim to satisfy by playing upon public fears and by creating structures of dependency. See *The Culture of Narcissism*, Warner Books, New York, 1979 p.385.
36 See D. Osborne & T. Gaebler *Reinventing Government*, Addison Wesley, Reading, Massachusetts 1992.

37 See Theo Mars, 'Public Sector Organization: Where Next?' *IDS Bulletin* (1992) vol. 23, No. 4, pp.18-30.

38 The necessity of such a reconciliation is a peculiarity of 'liberal' forms of government which must somehow intervene with 'non-interventionist' instruments. Accounting and audit appeal to liberal ideologies because, as apparently apolitical practices, they come to be recognised as necessary by social agents. See Nik Rose and Peter Miller 'Political Power beyond the State: Problematics of Government' *British Journal of Sociology* (1992, pp. 173-205.)

39 I would exclude tax inspection systems from the audit explosion despite the existence of PAYE and VAT audits. These practices have a longer history than the recent changes which I discuss. Tax inspection is primarily a form of direct monitoring for compliance with (the relatively unambiguous) rules which it serves. While it is certainly a disciplinary technology (See Alistair Preston, 'The Taxman Cometh: Some Observations on the Interrelationship between Accounting and Inland Revenue Practice', *Accounting, Organizations and Society*, 1989, pp.389-413), it has its own history. Furthermore, Inland Revenue practices have themselves become subject to the effects of the audit explosion in the public sector as inspection practices are required to demonstrate their 'value for money'.

40 The tendency of monitoring practices to shift towards a more indirect 'control of control' is internally paradoxical. It expresses both a recognition of the economic and epistemic impossibility of direct observational control at the same time as it reaffirms the *appearance* of control via the maintenance of systems integrity. This paradox is overcome by an epistemic shift in the concept of auditability. As first-order activities become increasingly unauditable within the existing portfolio of techniques, the audit shifts its focus towards second-order 'systems of control' which necessarily focus upon process.

41 This development of audit away from real-time forms of inspection conforms to certain postmodern motifs regarding 'loss of reference'. The primary reference point for auditing has become the evidential traces inscribed by systems of control which are increasingly formal in their structure and operation. The focus on systems means that audits may have less to do with control in a traditional direct sense and more to do with formalising the allocation of responsibility for systems integrity and process. For more on the construction of responsibility see Nils Brunsson, 'Deciding for Responsibility and Legitimation: Alternative Interpretations of Organizational Decision Making', *Accounting, Organizations and Society* 1990, pp.47-59, and Peter Miller, 'Accounting and Objectivity: The Invention of Calculable Selves and Calculable Spaces', *Annals of Scholarship, 1992, pp.61-86.*

42 In 'The Politics of Financial Auditing', *The Political Quarterly*, 1993, Vol 63, No. 3, pp. 272-284, I argue that responses to apparent failures in financial auditing are as much about avoiding inquiry into the technical efficacy of audit in general as they are about finding parties to blame. The institutional role of audit is thereby preserved.

43 See John Meyer and Brian Rowan, 'Institutionalised Organizations: Formal Structure as Myth and Ceremony', *American Journal of Sociology*, 1977, pp.340-363.

44 Patricia Day & Rudolf Klein, *Accountabilities: Five Public Services*, Tavistock, London 1987, p.174.

45 See Rose and Miller *op cit.*

46 See *Inquiry into the Supervision of the Bank of Credit and Commerce International*, HMSO, London, 1992.

47 See Christopher Humphrey et. al. *op cit.*

48 Any practice must have 'enough logic for the needs of practical behaviour, neither too much - since a certain vagueness is often indispensable, especially in negotiations - nor too little, since life would then become impossible', Pierre Bourdieu, 'From Rules to Strategies', in *Other Words: Essays towards a Reflexive Sociology* translated by Matthew Adamson, Polity Press, Cambridge 1990, p.73. Andrew Abbot makes a similar point when he remarks that professional knowledge must be 'abstract enough to survive small market shifts but not so abstract as to prevent monopoly' See *The System of Professions: An Essay on the Division of Expert Labour* University of Chicago Press, Chicago 1988, p.324.

49 International chamber of Commerce, *Effective Environmental Auditing*, ICC, Paris, 1991.

50 The recent European Community regulation relating to environmental management systems and audit distinguishes between 'environmental audit' as an internal affair and 'external verification' as a more independent form of scrutiny to establish that the conditions for registration are satisfied. The latter is vital to the credibility of the scheme and there are lessons to be learned from the quality assurance initiatives which provide the general model for environmental management. See 'Need a quality certificate? Ask Tom, Dick or Harry' *The Financial Times* March 8 1993; 'Standards Institute Defends Quality Management Benchmark' *The Financial Times* July 14 1993.

51 For example, recent concerns in the UK with the wording of financial audit reports, the only aspect of audit work which is publicly visible as a truncated and coded report, have been conducted in the name of improving communication. See Auditing Practices Board, *Proposals for an Expanded Audit Report*, APB, London, October 1991. The problem is particularly pertinent in the context of the auditor's opinion on whether an enterprise is a going concern. See Auditing Practices Board, *SAS 130 Exposure Draft - the Going Concern basis in Financial Statements*, London, APB, December 1993.

52 See Auditing Practices Board, *The Future Development of Auditing: A Paper to Promote Debate*, APB, London, November 1992; Cadbury Committee, *The Financial Aspects of Corporate Governance*, London 1992. Both these documents can be read as attempts to rethink audit in order to reconnect distant stakeholders to the inner workings of organisations. Audit is being shaped as the technology of corporate governance. However, it has been argued that these documents nevertheless reflect an accounting culture. See Judith Freedman, 'Accountants and Corporate Governance: Filling a Legal Vacuum' *The Political Quarterly*, 1993, pp.285-97.

53 Day and Klein *op cit* p.249.

54 These phrases are borrowed from Jürgen Habermas, 'The New Obscurity: The Crisis of the Welfare State and the Exhaustion of Utopian Energies', in Jürgen Habermas, *The New Conservatism: Cultural Criticism and the Historian's Debate* edited and translated by Shierry Weber Nicholsen, MIT Press, Cambridge MA, 1992, pp.48-70, and Gianni Vattimo, *The Transparent Society*, Polity Press, Cambridge, 1992. Habermas's diagnosis of the present impasse of the welfare state is instructive. Ideals of solidarity have given way to the regulatory logic of money and administrative power. In this sense the rise of audit is indicative of the exhaustion of utopian energies. Audits ensure accountability to individuals as 'clients' rather than citizens and it is no accident that the audit explosion has accompanied the displacement of older languages with that of markets, missions and management. These abstract concepts are mutually reinforcing.

55 See 'Tidal wave of dirty water' *The Financial Times* February 5 1994 which examines falling standards in the UK public sector.

56 In the 'Politics of Financial Auditing' I have formalised the problem of how the success of audit can be conceived. The problem is that it is impossible to disentangle successful auditing from successful company management and financial reporting. In the same way it is impossible to distinguish sharply between successful policing and other reasons for changing patterns of crime. Hence there is a certain asymmetry which underlies the politics of failure. Corporate failure will often give rise to public questions about financial audit failure. However, corporate success will not usually yield public approbation for the role of audit. It is in this sense that, as a matter of public perception, audits always fail. Only greater publicity about the process of audit could overcome this asymmetry.

57 An exception would be the financial savings claimed on behalf of value for money audits, although questions could always be raised about whether these were adequate. AC258 See Michael Power, 'Auditing and the Politics of Control in the UK Financial Services Sector' in J. McCahery, S. Picciotto and C. Scott (Eds) *Corporate Control and Accountability* , Clarendon Press, Oxford 1993, pp.187-202.

59 See Auditing Practices Board, *Proposed Statement of Auditing Standards - Exposure Draft 620 - The Auditors Right and Duty to Report to Regulators in the Financial Services Sector*, APB, London July 1993.

60 See also Ulrich Beck, 'From Industrial Society to Risk Society: Questions of Survival, Social Structure and Ecological Enlightenment', *Theory, Culture and Society* 1992, pp.97-123.

61 Early characterisations of the audit process consisted in the accountable party defending his actions in person to a relevant audience. The auditee was often visible throughout this process of defence but it was the aural as much as the observational intimacy which was the relevant parameter. Derived from the latin 'audire', early audits took the form of 'hearings' between auditor and auditee (See Peter Wolnizer, *Auditing as Independent Authentication*, Sydney University Press, Sydney, 1987 pp.35-39). Today, as modern financial audit practice has largely disengaged itself from these quasi-judicial origins, other bodies of knowledge have been invoked to shape the practice. Audit has emerged as a proto-scientific observational practice and, in North America in particular, aspirations to make audit 'properly scientific' have not entirely died away. Thus, while law has contributed the institutional context within which the demand for financial audits is shaped, the knowledge base of audit and the claims to expertise of its practitioners have become disengaged from their origins as a form of 'hearing' (although vestiges of these origins are to be found in the European Court of Auditors). Audit has emerged from the law to claim its own expertise and its attestation functions have come to develop an institutional momentum of their own.

62 Brendan McSweeney, 'Accounting for the Audit Commission', *Political Quarterly* Spring 1988 pp.28-43; also Day and Klein *op cit.*

63 See Carol Jones, 'Auditing criminal justice' *op cit.*

64 It must be said that VFM practitioners are aware of this issue - it does not happen behind their backs. See Peter Kimmance, 'The Widening Scope of Local Government Audit and Private Sector Participation' in A. Hopwood and C. Tomkins, *Issues in Public Sector Accounting* Phillip Allen, 1984, Oxford, pp.243-4.

65 See Ted Porter, 'Quantification and the Accounting Ideal in Science' *Social Studies of Science* (1992) Vol. 22, pp.633-52. Porter argues that the objectivity of accounting does not lie in its capability for accurate representation so much as its ability to provide a public and impartial medium.

66 Numerous articles have been published on this subject throughout 1992 and 1993 in the *Times Higher Education Supplement*.

67 For example, see 'Poor research: ranking blamed' *The Times Higher Educational Supplement* December 4 1993.

68 This has become embodied in the students' charter in which students are reconceived as having consumer rights. Such a programme depends crucially upon audit.

69 The UK Higher Education Funding Council has been exploring methods of making academic research expenditure more accountable and, in turn, auditable. Time sheets for academics have been proposed as a basis of making academic research auditable (See HEFC, *Accountability for Research Funds*, March 1993). In addition, pilot teaching quality audits have been conducted. One academic department was judged to be 'satisfactory' rather than 'excellent' largely because claims for excellence were not supported by sufficient evidence. This is indicative of the audit explosion and the shift from the substance of quality to the process of quality assurance has generated complaint: 'VCs reject quality red tape' *The Times Higher Educational Supplement* January 22 1993; 'Concern at pointless quality rules' *The Times Higher Educational Supplement* April 9 1993.

70 In this respect audit is consistent with Poster's concept of the 'superpanopticon' which constitutes its own system of self-reference while exerting a disciplining effect on the subject. Poster seems to attribute a disciplinary power to data bases as such whereas I would wish to implicate them within the specific practices of audit and surveillance which they make possible. See Mark Poster, *The Mode of Information*, Polity Press, Cambridge, 1990, chapter 3.

71 Audit may be a narcissistic practice which feeds off its own representations. It is a simulacrum in Baudrillard's sense. See Jean Baudrillard, *Simulations*, translated by Paul Foss et. al., Semiotext, New York, 1983.

72 See note 31 above.

73 See CEC DG XI/ UK Department of the Environment, *Research into the Development of Codes of Practice for Accredited Environmental Verifiers within the Framework of the Proposed Eco-management and Audit Regulation*, Judge Institute of Management Studies, Cambridge June 1993.

74 This image of audit knowledge would be disputed by financial audit practitioners and there is much discussion on this point. Some argue that checklists impose too much structure on the audit process and thereby inhibit professional judgement. However, practitioners will generally resist complete codification of their expertise in order to preserve its elite aura. Hence, debates about structure and judgement in the audit process have less of a purely technical character and have much to do with maintaining images of expertise.

75 Andrew Abbott, *op cit.*

76 Michael Power, 'From Common Sense to Expertise: Reflections on the Pre-history of Audit Sampling', *Accounting, Organizations and Society*, 1992 pp.37-62; Brian Carpenter and Mark Dirsmith, 'Sampling and the Abstraction of Knowledge in the Auditing Profession: An Extended Institutional Theory Perspective', *Accounting, Organizations and Society* 1993 pp 41-63.

77 See Stella Fearnley and Michael Page 'Audit Regulation - One Year On' *Accountancy*, January 1993 p.59. They observe that audit practitioners subjected to audit in this way have responded by standardising their 'official' audit approach in order to demonstrate technical competence. By doing so they tended to 'equate better files with better audits'. This is a consequence of the norm of auditability where even the 'audit of audit' requires that it be proceduralised. Results of the most recent audit of the auditors were available in early 1994 and can be interpreted both as failure and success. Failure because there seems to be a problem of audit quality for smaller practices, success because the critical stance of the monitoring agencies demonstrates their own independence.

78 It is important to emphasise that there is nothing conspiratorial about this. It is not, directly at least, a question of cartels and professional interests. Audit, as the 'self observation of the economic system' (Niklas Luhmann, *Ecological Communication* translated by J. Bednarz Polity Press, Cambridge, 1989) is a system of knowledge in its own right. It functions by virtue of an auditing logic which demands auditable auditees as the condition of possibility of its own functioning. The auditing system of knowledge 'productively misunderstands' (Gunther Teubner,

The Two Faces of Janus: Rethinking legal Pluralism *Cardozo Law Review* March 1992, Vol 13, No 5, pp.1443-62) the auditee in order to make it auditable. In turn, auditees are potentially alien disturbances to this system which reacts by rendering them familiar and auditable. But, if auditing is an autopoietic, self-sustaining practice it is itself the disturbing environment for auditees who may adapt their practices in the name of ideals of verifiability, calculability and responsible control (Peter Miller and Ted O'Leary, Accounting and the Construction of the Governable Person, *Accounting, Organizations and Society* 1987, pp.235-66). The key empirical question is how great is this submission to the audit process.

79 See Anthony Hopwood, 'Accounting and the Pursuit of Efficiency', in Anthony Hopwood and Cyril Tomkins, *Issues in Public Sector Accounting* Phillip Allan, Oxford 1984, pp.167-187. The overall effect is the displacement of non-accounting skills in public sector management.

80 See *The Henley Centre Planning for Social Change Survey 1992.*
81 See 'City warned of big increase in staff turnover' *The Financial Times* February 11 1994.
82 See William McInnes (ed) *Auditing into the Twenty First Century*, Institute of Chartered Accountants of Scotland, Edinburgh 1993. This document argues for a shift in emphasis from external to internal forms of audit. The danger in these innovative proposals is that if the internal audit function has been constructed as a mirror image of the external audit then the problems raised in this essay will be displaced but not solved.
83 This has always been the complaint by small companies. It is also becoming more evident in higher education. See, for example, 'Universities balk at review team costs' *The Times Higher Educational Supplement* September 17 1993.

84 See 'Council rejects quality advice' *The Times Higher Educational Supplement* February 18 1994. The Higher Education Quality Council has resisted advice from management consultants that its audit reports should be more explicitly critical. The consultants, Coopers & Lybrand, also suggest a move towards 'licensed auditors' with system-wide responsibilities analogous to financial auditors.

85 This is ironic in the light of post-Metallgesellschaft deliberations about the merits of UK audit committee arrangements over the German supervisory board structure. When the Cadbury proposals were first mooted in the UK, the German system was regarded by many as a preferable model. See 'Metallgesellschaft board "not at fault"' *The Financial Times* February 8 1994.

86 An interesting possibility is provided by *Public Concern at Work*, an independent centre resourced by the Joseph Rowntree Charitable Trust. Its aim is to facilitate structures which enable employees to register concerns about the conduct and standards of business.

87 Similar reservations about such charters have been expressed in 'Auditing the Accountants' *The Political Quarterly* Vol 64, No 3, p.270.

88 In the context of the United States, Johnson and Kaplan have argued that auditing has seriously inhibited the evolution of management accounting systems with damaging effects on competitiveness. See Thomas Johnson and Robert Kaplan, *Relevance Lost - The Rise and Fall of Management Accounting*, Harvard Business School, Harvard, 1987.

89 See Martin Trow, 'The Business of Learning' *The Times Higher Educational Supplement* October 8 1993.

90 See The Royal Society for the Encouragement of Arts, Manufactures & Commerce, *Tomorrow's Company*, RSA, London 1994.

ACKNOWLEDGEMENTS

I am very grateful to the following people for commenting upon earlier drafts of this paper: Andrew Barry, Nils Brunsson, Anthony Hopwood, John Law, John Meyer, Peter Miller, Brendan McSweeney, Geoff Mulgan, Christopher Napier, Keith Robson, Nikolas Rose, Brad Sherman, Claire Sinnott, Christopher Swinson, Lucy Zedner. Many others have provided invaluable comments at seminars and workshops.

Demos

Demos is an independent think-tank set up to improve the breadth and quality of political and policy debate. It encourages radical thinking and solutions to the long-term problems facing the UK and other advanced industrial societies. It brings together thinkers and doers.

Demos is a registered charity. It is financed by voluntary donations from individuals, foundations and companies.

The views expressed in publications are those of the authors alone. They do not represent Demos' institutional viewpoint.

If you wish to support Demos' activities, you can become a subscriber. Further details available from Demos' offices; 9 Bridewell Place, London EC4V 6AP. Telephone: 071-353 4479.

Other Demos publications available for £5.95 post free from Demos, 9 Bridewell Place, London EC4V 6AP.

Reconnecting Taxation by Geoff Mulgan and Robin Murray

Geoff Mulgan is Director of Demos. Robin Murray is a Fellow of the Institute of Development Studies at Sussex University.

ISBN 1 898309 00 0

An End to Illusions by Alan Duncan

Alan Duncan is Conservative MP for Rutland and Melton. He entered the House of Commons in 1992.

ISBN 1 898309 05 1

Transforming the Dinosaurs by Sir Douglas Hague

Sir Douglas Hague is an Associate Fellow of Templeton College, Oxford, non-executive director of CRT Group plc and President of Corporate Positioning Services.

ISBN 1 898309 10 8

The Parenting Deficit by Amitai Etzioni

Amitai Etzioni is Professor of Sociology at George Washington University. He has previously worked at Harvard Business School, the Brookings Institution and the White House.

ISBN 1 898309 20 5

Sharper Vision by Ian Hargreaves

Ian Hargreaves is Deputy Editor of the Financial Times. He was formerly Head of News and Current Affairs at the BBC.

ISBN 1 898309 25 6

The World's New Fissures by Vincent Cable

Vincent Cable is Director of the International Economics Programme at the Royal Institute for International Affairs.

ISBN 1 898309 35 3

Demos also produces a Quarterly magazine which is priced at £2.50 (£3 inc p&p) and has so far featured special issues on unemployment and education.